PLANET SOS

FRAGILE PLANET

Gerry Bailey

Gareth Stevens Publishing

Please visit our Web site, www.garethstevens.com. For a free color catalog of all our high-quality books, call toll free 1-800-542-2595 or fax 1-877-542-2596.

Library of Congress Cataloging-in-Publication Data

Bailey, Gerry.
Fragile planet / Gerry Bailey.
p. cm. — (Planet SOS)
Includes index.
ISBN 978-1-4339-4974-6 (lib. bdg.)
ISBN 978-1-4339-4975-3 (pbk.)
ISBN 978-1-4339-4976-0 (6-pack)
1. Natural disasters—Juvenile literature. I. Title.
GB5019.B345 2011
363.34—dc22

2010032886

Published in 2011 by
Gareth Stevens Publishing
111 East 14th Street, Suite 349
New York, NY 10003

Designer: Simon Webb
Editor: Felicia Law

Printed in the United States of America

CPSIA compliance information: Batch #CW11GS: For further information contact Gareth Stevens, New York, New York at 1-800-542-2595.

CONTENTS

VOLCANO ALERT

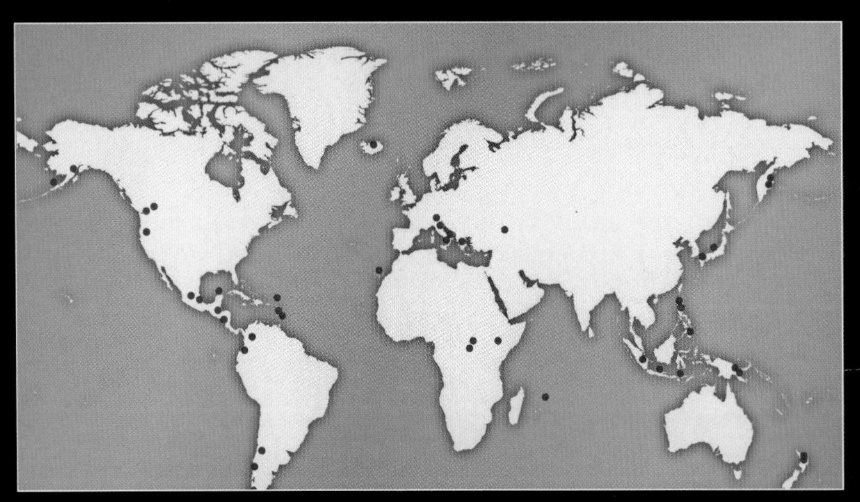

Where do you find volcanoes?

The red dots on the map show where the largest active volcanoes in the world are located.

Not just another mountain

You might mistake a volcano for just another mountain. But it's not. A volcano can be dangerous. That's because volcanoes can explode, or erupt.

When this happens, very hot, semiliquid rock, known as lava, spews out of its cone-shaped top. To add to this, fast-moving clouds of dust, poisonous gases, and ash can shoot out as well. Anything in the path of this destructive mix is in real danger.

Volcanic bombs

A volcanic bomb is a large lump of cooled lava, often shaped like a ball. The force of the eruption can throw these bombs many miles away, making them dangerous. In 1993, some people were killed by lava bombs when the Galeras Volcano in Colombia, South America, erupted unexpectedly.

Volcanic activity

Volcanoes that erupt regularly are described as "active."

Those that erupt very occasionally, perhaps never in living memory, are called "dormant."

Those that no longer erupt are known as "extinct."

The "great escape"

The surface of Earth is actually a thin crust of rock floating on a bed of molten rock, known as magma. Like when you peel the skin from an orange, Earth's crust is made up of several large and smaller pieces, called tectonic plates.

The molten rock is made liquid by the terrific heat at Earth's center. The closer to the center the magma moves, the hotter it becomes. The intense heat also makes it lighter, and it starts to rise, heading for the surface. If it can find a crack in Earth's crust, it will escape. We call this "great escape" a volcanic eruption.

When gas gets trapped in the lava it makes it "frothy." When it cools it forms a lightweight rock known as pumice.

A cross-section of a volcano.

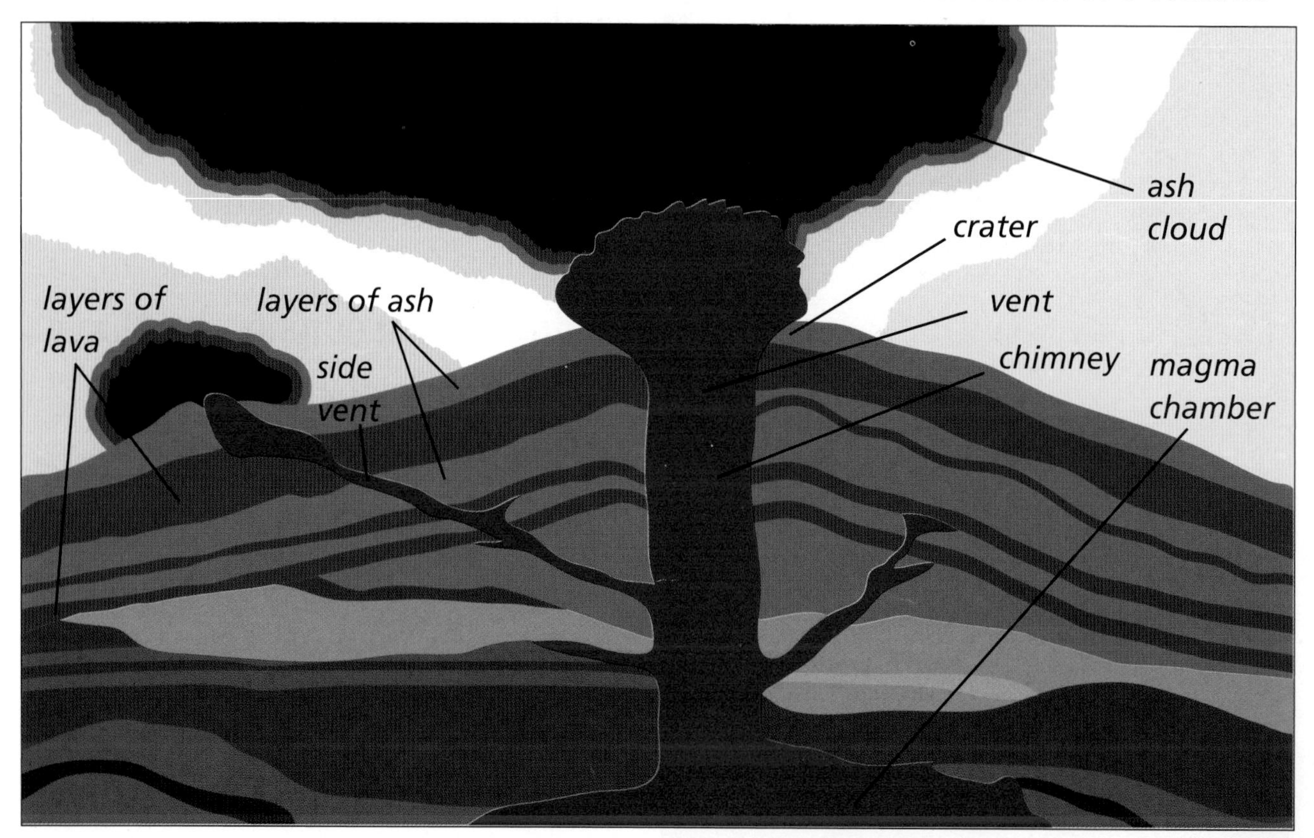

Lava flows downhill at around the speed of a jogger.

Magma to lava

The easiest way for magma to escape is through a natural crack in Earth's surface. Cracks like this happen along the lines where tectonic plates meet and are at their weakest. As it rises, the magma spills outwards – where it is known as lava – then cools and hardens. It forms a cone shape on the surface that we call a volcano.

Supervolcanoes

Most volcanoes are not hard to spot. They are the shape of a normal hill or mountain but with a dented summit. But some volcanoes are not so easy to see. These are the supervolcanoes.

Underground explosion

The reason that supervolcanoes are hard to find is that they are underground. In fact, most are under the sea. Magma rises and flows into a huge underground chamber, where the pressure and heat start to build. Eventually the surrounding crust gives way and lava, ash, and poisonous gases explode in every direction through any gap they can find – at high speed.

Supervolcanoes often form circular basins, or calderas. This happens when the empty chamber can no longer support the weight of the mountain above it, so the top collapses inward.

This caldera in California has filled with water, forming a lake.

A famous supervolcano

Yellowstone is a national park in the United States. It's also a supervolcano. The park rests on top of a huge caldera of molten rock 45 miles (72 km) across and 8 miles (13 km) deep. It's called a hotspot – and for good reason. Yellowstone National Park is likely to erupt sometime in the next 10,000 years, and could destroy a large part of the United States.

The heat from the magma chamber has caused hot pools, hot springs and bubbling mud pots to form, as well as boiling fountains of water known as geysers.

This geyser in the park is a famous one known as Old Faithful.

Living with a volcano

You might think that given the danger, people wouldn't want to live too near a volcano. But they do. That's because volcanic soil is very fertile and therefore good for growing things.

Mount Merapi is one of the most active volcanoes in Indonesia, and people have been farming its slopes for hundreds of years. Because it erupts so often, the sides of the volcano are covered in ash, creating excellent farmland.

Merapi erupts every two or three years, but the last really big eruption was in 2006, when tens of thousands of villagers had to leave their homes.

Mount Merapi towers over rice fields in Indonesia.

THE EARTH QUAKES

The San Andreas Fault runs for more than 800 miles (1,300 km) through California.

Moving plates

Earth's crust is made up of segments, called tectonic plates. Each of these is slowly moving over a bed of molten magma. Where these plates meet, there are often weak zones in the crust, called faults. These faults are where earthquakes are likely to happen. Hundreds of earthquakes jolt our planet every day.

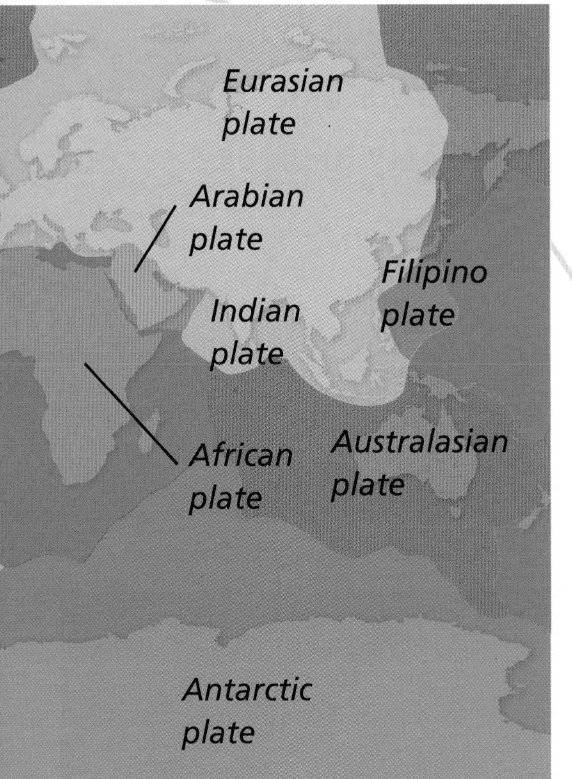

Each colored section shows a different tectonic plate.

The moving plates push and grind against one another. This pushing occurs over thousands of years, but when one plate suddenly shifts, it causes an earthquake. Smaller movements are known as tremors.

Shock waves

An earthquake releases energy in the form of seismic waves, which radiate from the point underground where the earthquake occurs, called the focus. Surface waves spread out from the epicenter, a point on Earth's surface directly above the focus. It is these surface waves that cause the most damage.

An aftershock is the shaking or tremor that occurs after the main earthquake. Aftershocks can happen minutes, hours or even months after the first shock of the earthquake.

Spreading waves

When an earthquake happens it sends waves of energy through the earth. These waves are called seismic waves and they spread out from the focus of the earthquake.

Scientists who study earthquakes are called seismologists. They gather data about seismic waves to give information about earthquakes. And as earthquakes often come before a volcanic eruption, they can use the information they gather to try to predict when both might happen.

A seismograph

Scientists studying seismic waves use an instrument called a seismograph. It measures how much the ground shakes or vibrates during an earthquake.

A pen attached to a spring records the strength of the seismic waves on a roll of paper fixed to a rotating drum. When a wave is detected the pen creates a pattern of peaks and troughs on the paper.

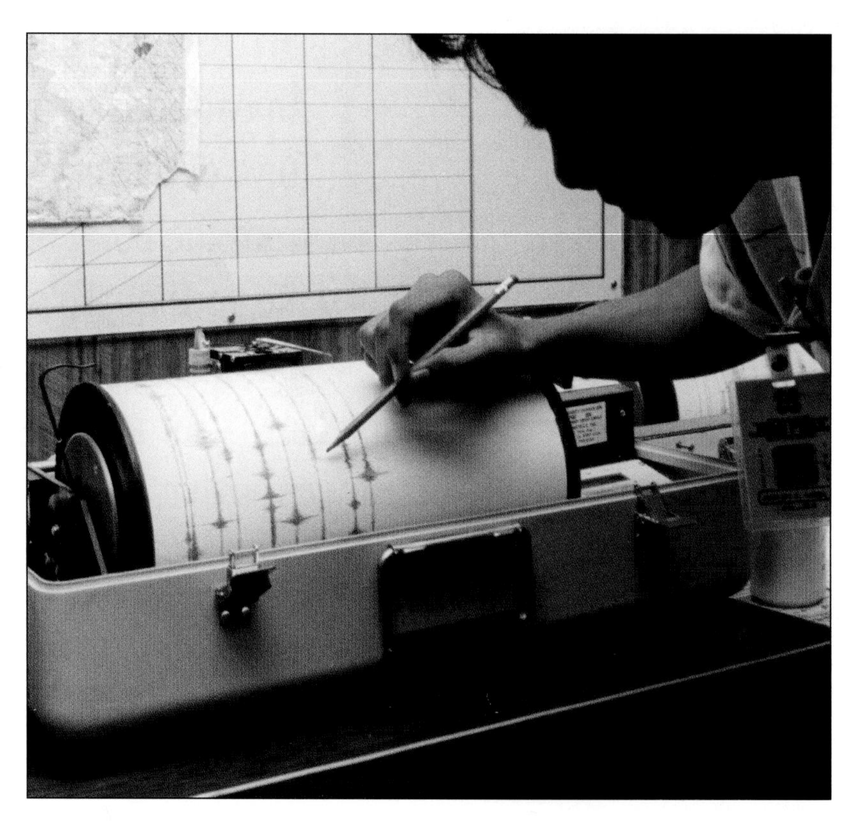

A seismograph prints out a seismic chart.

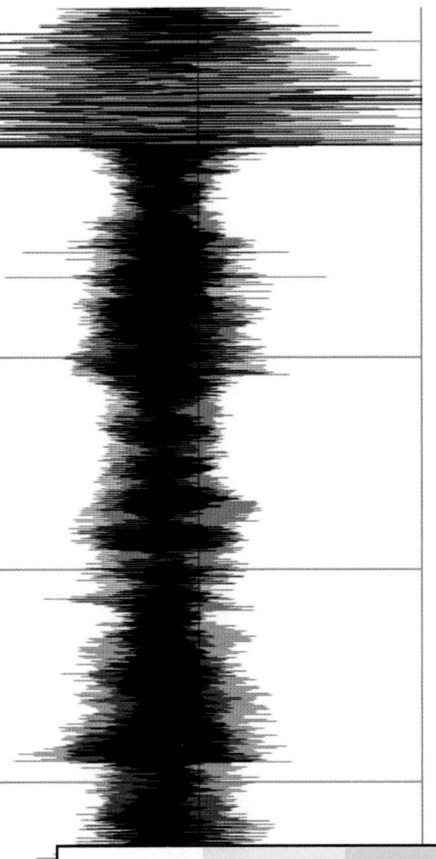

The Richter scale

Seismographs detect tremors and earthquakes and are also used to measure their size and location. Most people have heard of the Richter scale, which was developed by an American seismologist named Charles Richter in the 1930s. It measures the size of an earthquake according to the amount of energy released – known as its magnitude. The scale can be used to compare the size of one earthquake with another.

The Richter scale

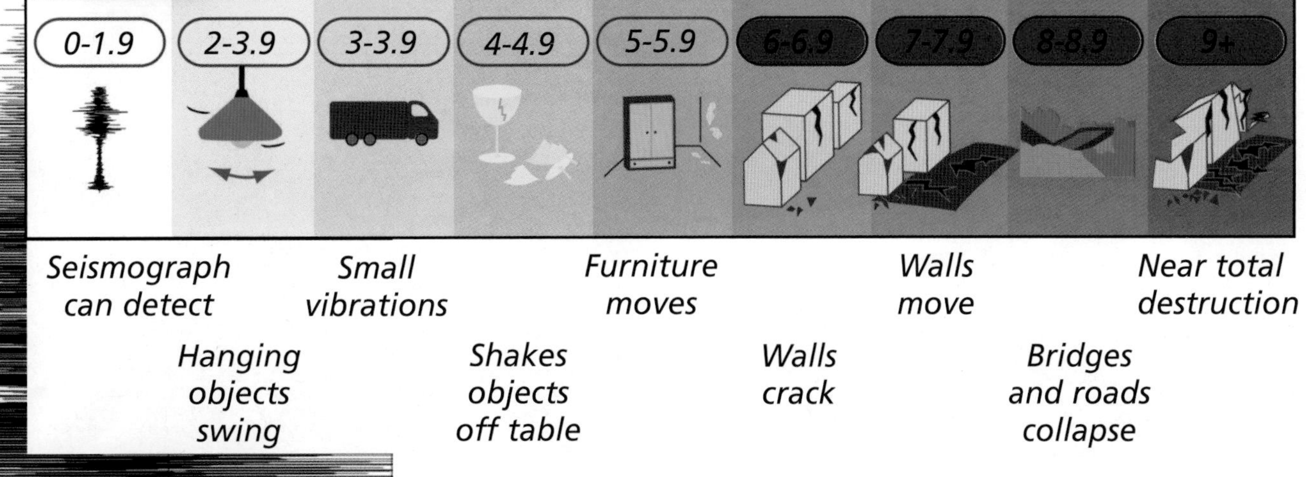

Moment magnitude

Today, most seismologists prefer to use a more accurate measurement: the moment magnitude scale. This measures how much energy is released when the plates slip. An earthquake is described as "magnitude 4," or whatever number it is. Magnitude 9 is a very severe earthquake.

Buildings and property were totally destroyed in the Sichuan earthquake.

Tumbling cities

Cities and towns are made up of buildings that are often closely packed together. There are few open spaces so when an earthquake happens, buildings will collapse onto each other.

Any strong vibration through the ground will cause damage. In an earthquake zone, buildings need to be built so they can absorb a shock – so they can shake or move just a little on their foundations. If this is not the case, then the walls and roofs of buildings will quickly dislodge, crack and finally break up and fall.

China's worst earthquake

On May 12, 2008, an 8.0 magnitude earthquake hit the Eastern Sichuan province in China. The closest large city to the epicenter, 37 miles (60 km) away, was Dujiangyan. It suffered major damage. Thousands of its buildings collapsed, including schools and hospitals. Overall, nearly 70,000 people were killed in Sichuan.

Rescue was made difficult because landslides caused by the quake blocked roads. More damage was done by aftershocks, which continued for weeks after the first earthquake.

Schoolchildren practice earthquake drills in class.

Quake proof

You'd think that once an area was known for its earthquake activity, people might just pack up and leave. But about 600 million people prefer to stay put. They have jobs or family that make it difficult to move. Lots of children around the world must learn what to do if an earthquake strikes. Here are some tips:

Before an earthquake:

- Practice moving to a safe place away from windows.
- Have an emergency plan to contact your family if you get separated.
- Prepare an emergency kit, with flashlight, first aid supplies, radio, food, and water.

During an earthquake:

- Take cover under a table.
- Stay away from glass, windows, or furniture that could fall, such as a bookcase.
- If you're in bed, stay where you are and protect your head with a pillow.
- Do not move outside – it's more dangerous. If you're outside already, move away from buildings and street lights.

Stop the shaking!

One of the tasks facing architects is how to produce buildings that are quake proof. Many great cities are built in earthquake zones, including Tokyo, Los Angeles, and Mexico City. Here the buildings must be built to withstand frequent earth tremors as well as occasional really bad quakes.

Bend and stretch

Earthquake-proof buildings need to be made of very strong materials that can bend, stretch, and squeeze without breaking. One method is to belt the building all around using steel bands that allow beams to move but not buckle. Also, friction plates in the walls and foundations slide over each other when shaken instead of rubbing and weakening.

The Transamerica Pyramid, a skyscraper in San Francisco, was built to resist quakes. It withstood an earthquake in 1989 that caused billions of dollars' worth of damage to other buildings in the surrounding area.

The movement of the skier dislodges the loose surface snow but also causes a crack in the packed snow beneath.

AVALANCHE!

Imagine an enormous, thundering mountain of snow tumbling towards you – it's an avalanche! As snow falls on a mountainside it builds up in layers. These layers, like everything else on the planet, are pulled downwards by force of gravity. The heavier the layers of snow get, the more likely they are to start sliding down the mountain.

Most avalanches are made up of slabs or plates of snow, rather than loose snow. Slab avalanches reach speeds of 56 to 75 miles (90 to 120 km) an hour. The slide might start gently, but as the mass of snow travels downwards, it quickly gathers speed and also picks up more snow.

Snow fences can stop snow or at least slow its movement. Smaller, controlled avalanches can be deliberately set off by explosives. This moves the loose snow before it can move itself.

A search and rescue helicopter in action.

Mountain rescue

Anyone who travels to snowy, mountainous areas is at risk. Skiers, climbers, and snowmobilers – even people who are just walking in the hills – can be caught by sudden changes in the weather, by an accident, by getting lost, or by not being properly prepared.

Most popular mountain areas have dedicated rescue teams on standby, who are ready to deal with emergencies. Where necessary, helicopters are used because they can get to areas too remote for other forms of transport. They carry medical staff and rush the injured back to hospital.

Rescue dogs

Dogs have a great sense of smell, far better than that of a human. They're also intelligent. So some breeds are trained to work with rescue teams. It takes more than a year to train each dog and costs a lot of money. The dogs are trained to find traces of human scent drifting in the air, and then to move where the scent is most concentrated. During an earthquake in Mexico City, dogs found eight people alive who had been missing for five days.

St. Bernard dogs are bred in the mountains of Switzerland. For hundreds of years they were the symbol of mountain rescue, although they are rarely used to do this work today.

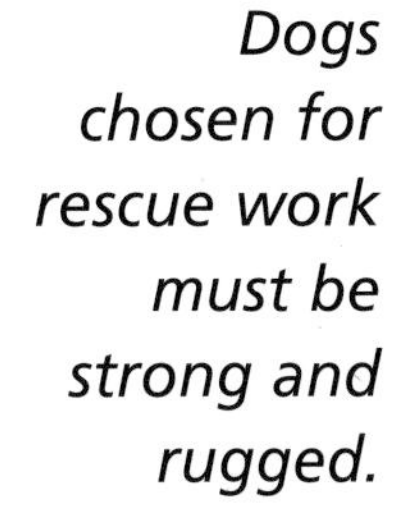

Dogs chosen for rescue work must be strong and rugged.

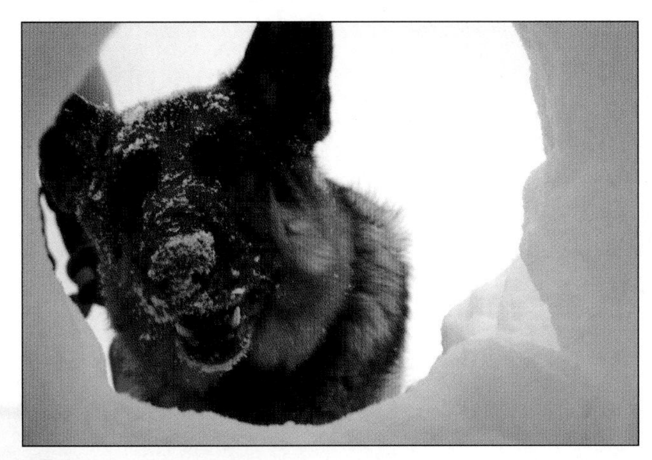

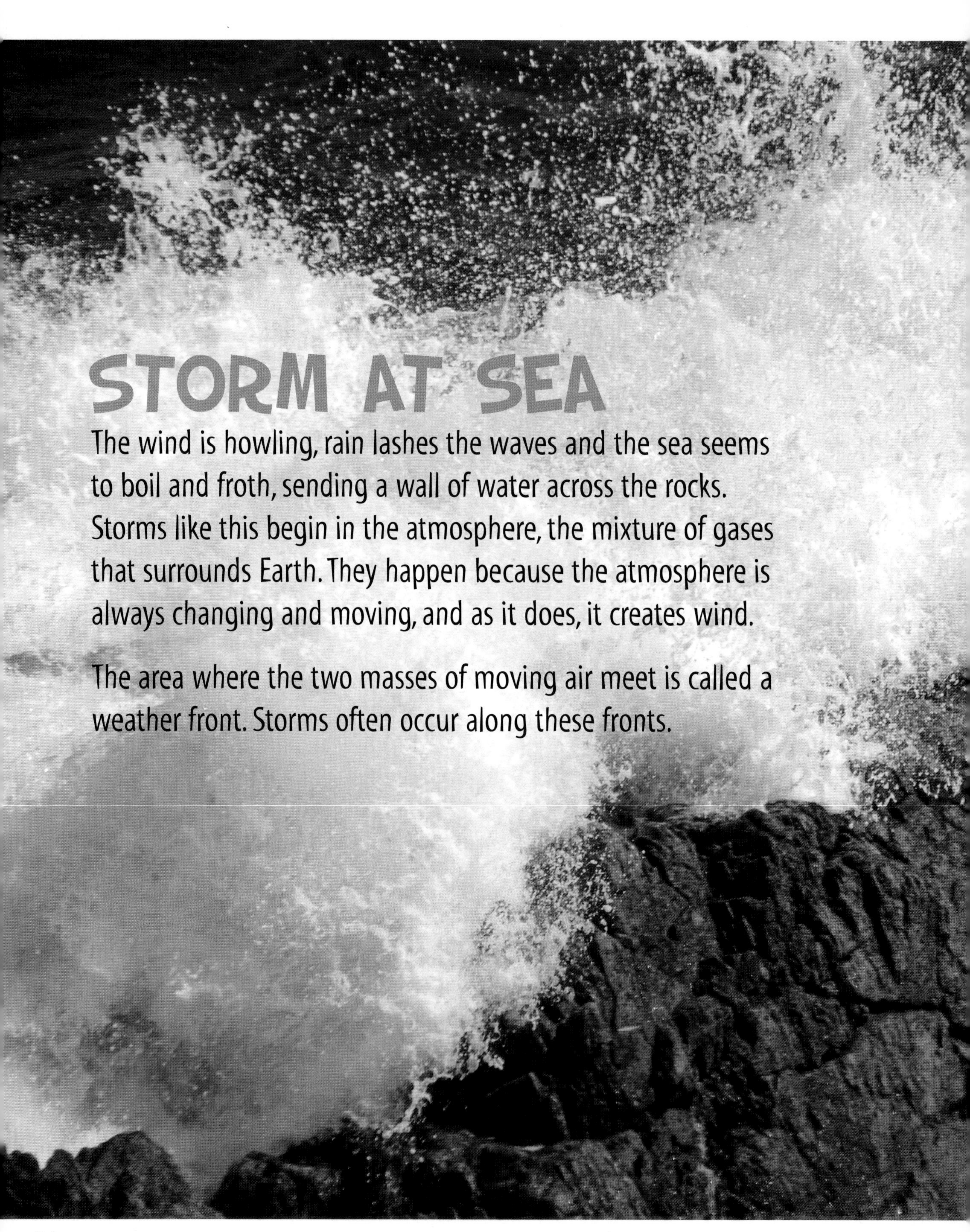

STORM AT SEA

The wind is howling, rain lashes the waves and the sea seems to boil and froth, sending a wall of water across the rocks. Storms like this begin in the atmosphere, the mixture of gases that surrounds Earth. They happen because the atmosphere is always changing and moving, and as it does, it creates wind.

The area where the two masses of moving air meet is called a weather front. Storms often occur along these fronts.

Weather fronts

Our atmosphere can change in different ways. If the humidity, the amount of water in it, goes down or up, it will seem either dry or damp. Its temperature can change and, very importantly, the air pressure can change too. As masses of air move around, they bump into other masses of air that might have a different humidity, temperature, or pressure.

Air pressure is the amount of force produced as air presses down on the land or sea below. The warmer the air, the lighter it is.

Storms can produce balls of frozen water such as these huge hailstones.

Sea rescue

When someone is in trouble at sea they may send out an SOS message for help. Specially trained search and rescue teams pick up the message. These emergency teams use helicopters as well as lifeboats to find and rescue people in distress. The work can be dangerous because rescues are often carried out in high winds and rough seas.

A person is winched up to an Air-Sea Rescue helicopter.

Lifeboats like this one patrol the seas and oceans of the world.

Ocean Ranger disaster

Oil rigs are like huge stationary ships at sea that are set up to drill for oil and natural gas trapped in the rocks of the seabed. They are anchored to the floor of the ocean.

A Coast Guard boat takes a battering from high seas during a storm.

On February 14, 1982, a terrible storm blew up off the coast of Newfoundland, Canada. At the time, the Ocean Ranger was the mightiest oil rig in the world, and it lay in the path of the storm. As tall as a 35-story building, the rig was built to withstand the severest storms. But not this one! Pounded by waves of up to 65 feet (20 m) high, a broken porthole started to let in water.

As the storm reached its height the great rig began to tip. Then it capsized. Rescue attempts by the Coast Guard were made impossible by the weather. All 84 men aboard were killed.

Tsunami warning sign.

KILLER WAVES

A tsunami is a series of huge waves, usually caused by an earthquake under the sea. But it can also be triggered by volcanic eruptions and underwater landslides.

A tsunami usually starts deep under the surface of the sea and isn't really noticeable until it comes thundering onto the shore. Out at sea, it just appears as a hump in the surface. Tsunami waves travel at great speed, between 310 and 620 miles (500 and 1,000 km) per hour, and can travel long distances. Only when they reach the shore do they slow down and gain height.

The 2004 tsunami breaks on the shore in Thailand.

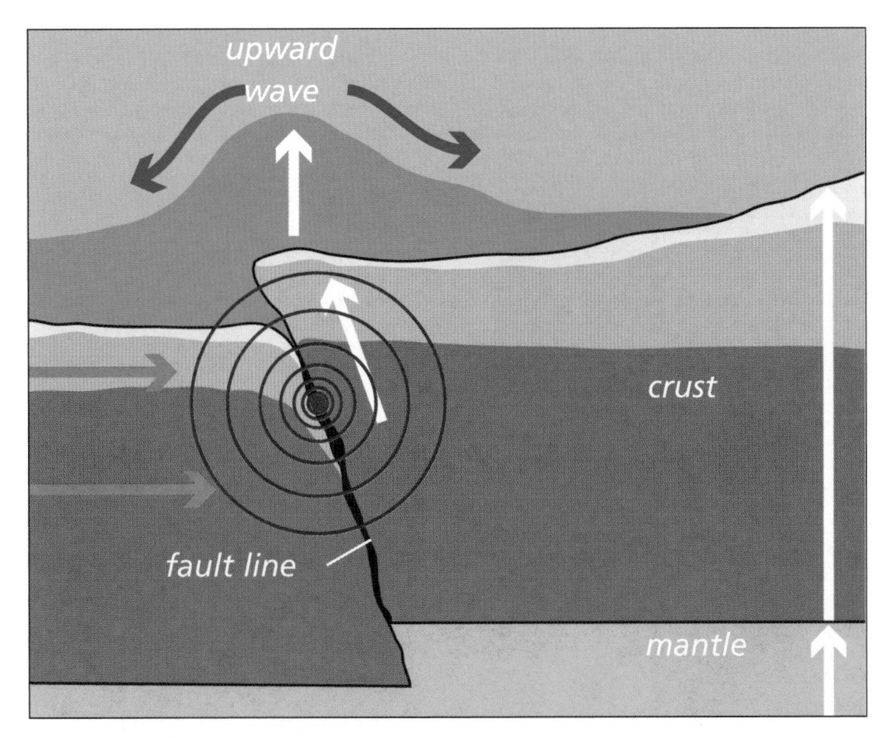

The tectonic plates collide at the fault line, creating an undersea earthquake. This causes a backward–forward movement in the water, and a huge wave results.

Warning!

It's not easy to predict when a tsunami will occur. Scientists use radar satellites that monitor sea levels for any unusual rise or fall. They also use special equipment out at sea that measures sea levels as well as temperature and air pressure.

Harbor wave

Around 200 tsunamis have been recorded in Japan's history. The name means "harbor wave," and was used because Japanese fishermen returning from the open sea would sometimes find their harbor and nearby buildings all demolished by a huge wave, although they hadn't seen anything extraordinary out at sea. Mistakenly, they thought the wave had occurred only in the harbor, so they gave it this name.

Reporting stations are set up on the surface of the deep seas to measure changes in the oceans' behavior.

The Indian Ocean Tsunami

On December 26, 2004, a massive earthquake under the Indian Ocean set off a huge movement of the sea. A wall of water swept towards the coast of Indonesia and other Asian countries. At its highest the main wave reached 108 feet (33 m), making it one of the biggest waves ever known.

A great shift

The earthquake that caused the tsunami was the second largest ever recorded. It had a moment magnitude between 9.1 and 9.3.

It was so powerful that it caused the whole Earth to wobble on its axis by almost an inch (2.5 cm). It may even have shortened the day by slightly changing the Earth's shape. It also caused some islands to move.

This series of great waves became known as the Indian Ocean Tsunami. It was caused when the India tectonic plate slid about 50 feet (15 m) under the Burma plate and ruptured, or split, along almost 1,000 miles (1,600 km) of its length. The tsunami caused enormous devastation and killed more than 250,000 people.

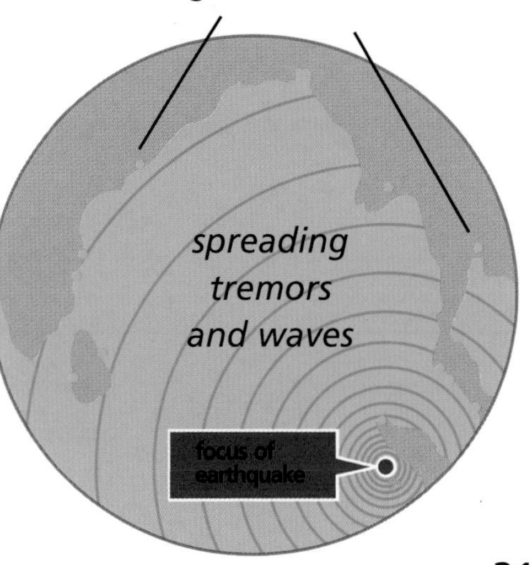

SLIDING LAND

When land collapses and starts to move, it can cause massive destruction. Land on slopes may be triggered to slide downhill by an earth tremor, by erosion caused by the weakening of tree roots in the soil, or even by a strong wind. But often the cause is heavy rain, in which case the land slides down as heavy mud.

Mudslides are fast-moving landslides that flow downhill in channels. They usually begin on steep slopes, growing bigger as water builds up in the ground, creating liquid mud. Anything that shakes the earth will cause the mud to move—up to 50 miles (80 km) an hour.

Tree roots will hold the soil in place while the ground is stable. But heavy rain quickly washes it away.

Mudslides can happen quickly, threatening land and property.

A landslide must be cleared away before the road can reopen.

Mudslides also cause other problems. They stop all the important services, such as electricity, water, gas supply, and sewage lines. The damage to roads or railways can halt traffic and stop help from getting to the area.

HIGH WINDS

We can't see it, but we can hear it and really feel it. It's traveling at nearly 100 miles (160 km) per hour. It's the wind. The air, or atmosphere, is constantly moving. Sometimes it moves gently but at other times it moves ferociously and can cause terrible natural disasters. High winds are simply masses of air moving very quickly. We call them cyclones, tornadoes, hurricanes, typhoons, gales, or other names, depending on how they act and where they are located.

As well as creating high winds, the moisture that the hurricane picks up falls again as torrential rain. Out at sea, hurricane winds also whip up the seawater to create a huge wave called a storm surge, which can cause floods.

Small tornadoes known as dust devils are whipped up by light winds in the desert.

Huge hurricanes

Hurricanes are probably the most destructive of high winds. They cause the largest storms and can do tremendous damage. In the Asia-Pacific region, hurricanes are known as typhoons.

Hurricanes start life over warm seas or oceans. As the air becomes hotter it begins to rise. As it rises it sucks up air from below and this air begins to swirl around like a giant wheel because of the rotation of Earth. As it swirls the wind moves faster and faster, and can reach speeds of up to 185 miles (300 km) per hour. The center of the wheel is calm, and is known as the eye.

Weather satellites, high in space, help to detect hurricanes and plot their movement.

Whirling winds

Tornadoes, or twisters, are fierce, spinning columns of wind with speeds of 250 miles (400 km) an hour or more. They develop out of thunderstorms, and a leaden grey sky, heavy hail and the roar of thunder are often signs that a tornado is on its way. They can occur almost anywhere in the world, but are especially common in the Great Plains, in an area known as Tornado Alley.

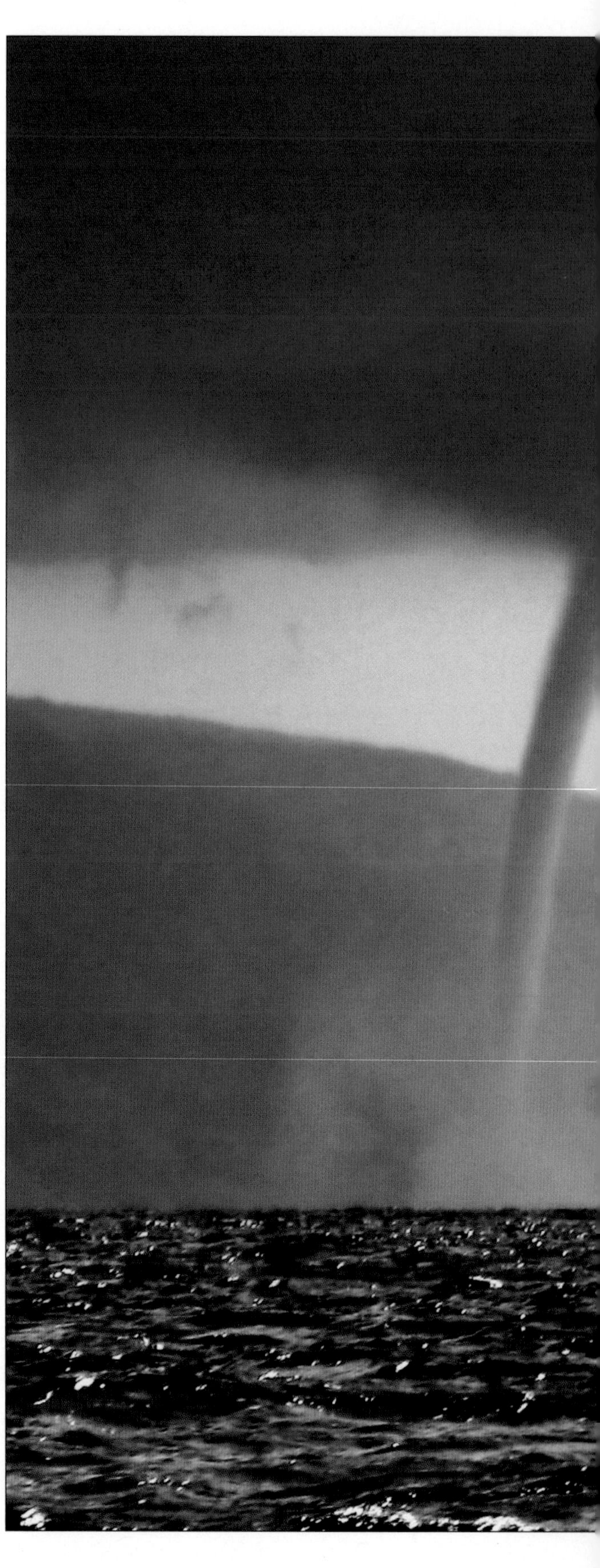

These rounded clouds, called mammatus clouds, are a warning sign that a tornado may form.

This anvil-shaped cloud, a cumulonimbus, is typical of thunderstorm clouds.

There are around 1,200 tornadoes in the United States every year.

Tri-state Twister

Twisters are most common in spring, when the weather is warming up. The world's most devastating tornado occurred in the United States in March 1925.

Known as the Tri-state Twister, this killer storm sped through the states of Missouri, Illinois, and Indiana, covering more than 215 miles (350 km), and traveling at a speed of 60 miles (100 km) an hour.

The Tri-state Twister was described as "a rolling mass of boiling clouds." It caused the deaths of nearly 700 people.

LIGHTNING STRIKE

In any 24-hour period, some 40,000 thunderstorms take place around the globe. Lightning is an impressive phenomenon, especially when it happens at night. And as about 100 bolts of it strike the ground every second, it can be extremely dangerous too.

A flash of lightning can destroy anything in its path, from a tree to a human being. It contains a huge amount of power – one bolt can contain up to a billion volts of electricity – and can reach temperatures five times hotter than the surface of the sun. The shock waves it creates are what we hear as thunder.

Lighting up the sky

Some kinds of lightning never leave the clouds. They travel between differently charged areas, from one cloud to another, or flash inside them. A bolt of lightning flickers as the electricity rushes between the negatively charged clouds and the positively charged ground, traveling at speeds of up to 62,000 miles (100,000 km) per second.

A bolt of lightning makes a spectacular display in the night sky.

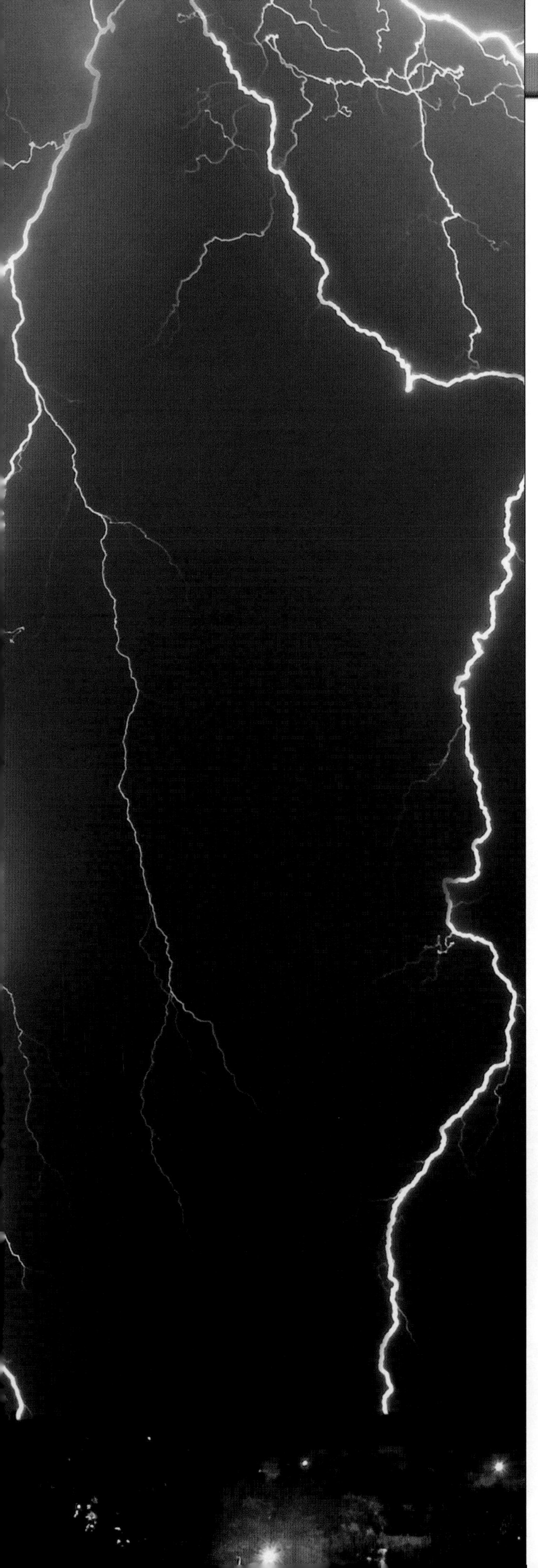

What makes lightning?

When clouds form they build up positive and negative electrical charges. During a storm, particles of rain, snow, or ice inside the cloud collide with each other.

This causes the bottom part of the cloud to have a negative charge and the top part a positive one.

When the negatively charged area starts to get overloaded, a shaft of negative electrons reaches down to the ground, while a shaft of positive ones reaches up to meet it.

What makes lightning happen?

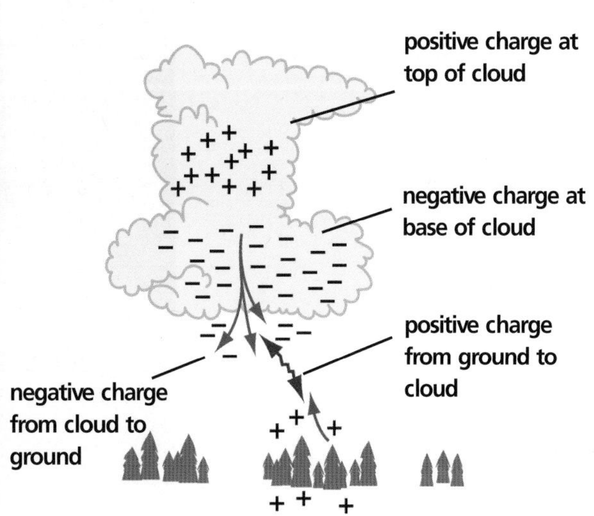

RED CROSS, RED CRESCENT

When natural disasters happen, such as the Indian Ocean Tsunami, people turn to relief organizations such as the Red Cross and the Red Crescent for help. Anyone who needs protection or assistance in coping with situations ranging from famine to earthquakes can call on them. They are there for everyone regardless of color, religion, or nationality.

Their goal is to reduce the number of deaths and injuries from natural or man-made disasters and to relieve the health emergencies and outbreaks of disease that often follow. They work to increase the ability of local communities to cope in really urgent situations. Importantly, they promote respect for all human beings and work to reduce intolerance and discrimination.

Emergency organizations set up and run campsites like this one at the scene of a disaster.

Red Cross and Red Crescent relief workers unload aid packages.

A helping hand

A Swiss businessman, Henry Dunant, traveled to Italy in June 1859. He saw the terrible suffering of soldiers at the Battle of Solferino and was shocked that there was no organized medical group to take care of them. He stayed to help. Back in Switzerland, in 1863 he and four others set up the organization that would become the Red Cross. Today, the Red Cross/Red Crescent Movement has around 97 million volunteers, supporters and staff, and operates in 186 countries.

The Red Crescent symbol was recognized as equal to the Red Cross in 1929. Today it is the emblem used by 33 countries with mainly Muslim populations.

The flags of the Red Cross and the Red Crescent fly together above an aid center.

HELPING HAND

Our planet is clearly a very vulnerable and very precious place. Even the smallest changes can develop into a global problem. It may seem as if a tsunami or a hurricane that happens many thousands of miles away has nothing to do with us. But the truth is that we are all crowded onto a very small area of Earth's crust, and any strong ground, sea, or air movements eventually affect us all in one way or another.

Of course, we can't influence the planet's behavior – but we can make sure that the land and sea and air are as clean and undisturbed as we can keep them. Everyone can do something. Here are some of the things we and others can do to help.

1. Don't trash it!

Recycle all your empty household containers – glass, plastic, paper, and metal.

2. Use your own shopping bag

Plastic bags are not biodegradable and end up polluting our rivers and seas.

3. Try something different

It takes 40 times as much water to produce 2.2 pounds (1 kg) of meat as it does to produce 2.2 pounds (1 kg) of vegetables. Go vegetarian once a week, support local growers and help save global resources.

4. Bring a mug

Don't use paper or polystyrene cups – have your own favorite mug and stop the waste.

Learn basic first aid

Find out about classes for your age group so you can deal with simple injuries.

Restock!

Floods are essential to farming because they bring water and nutrients to regenerate the soil and refill underground water supplies.

Rebuild and rehouse

Major disasters may cause devastation but they also present opportunities for a fresh start. Bad housing can be replaced with more modern accommodations.

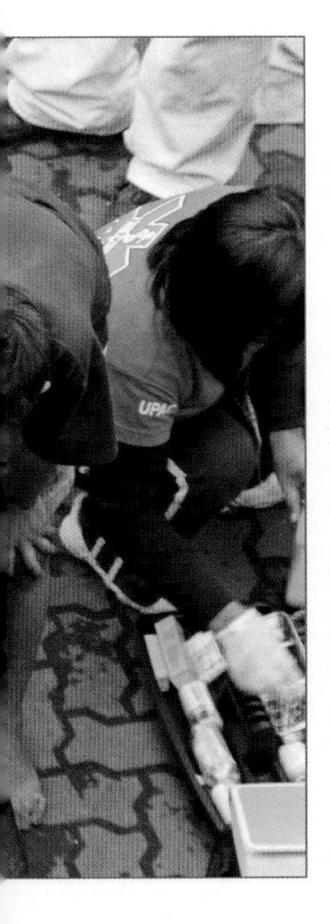

Replant!

Volcanoes may be dangerous, but there is a positive benefit to farmers on the island of Lanzarote and elsewhere, who farm the fertile volcanic lava. Plants grow quickly and well in the soil, which is rich in minerals.

GLOSSARY

aftershock A tremor (often one of a series) occurring after the main shock of an earthquake.

air pressure The weight of the air in the atmosphere pressing down on Earth.

atmosphere The layer of gases surrounding Earth, or other planets or stars.

avalanche The rapid flow of snow down a slope, caused either by a natural event or by human activity.

caldera A large crater formed by a volcanic explosion or by the collapse of the cone of a volcano.

chimney (volcano) The central hole in a volcano up through which the lava erupts.

crater A bowl-shaped geological formation at the top of a volcano.

crust (Earth) The hard outer layer of Earth.

cumulonimbus A tall, dark cloud that is charged with electricity and associated with thunderstorms and other intense weather.

dust devil A miniature whirlwind formed in hot, dry conditions, strong enough to whip up dust and sand.

earthquake A sudden movement of Earth's crust that causes the land to shift

environment The surrounding area in which plants and animals live.

epicenter The point on Earth's surface directly above the focus of an earthquake.

eruption A sudden, violent discharge of steam and volcanic material.

eye The still, central point of a hurricane.

famine A severe food shortage resulting in hunger, starvation, and even death.

fault A crack in Earth's crust between two or more tectonic plates.

flood An overflowing of seawater or freshwater over land that is usually dry.

friction The resistance encountered when one object or surface rubs against another.

Galeras Volcano An active volcano in southwest Colombia.

gas Matter that is not in a solid or liquid state.

geyser A natural hot spring that ejects a fountain of water and steam into the air.

gravity The force of attraction that pulls objects towards Earth's core.

hailstones Small, rounded pellets of ice that fall during a thunderstorm.

humidity The amount of water vapor or wetness in the atmosphere.

hurricane A severe, rotating storm, usually with heavy rains and high-speed winds.

landslide The sliding movement of a large mass of earth and rock down a mountain, cliff or hillside.

lava Molten rock expelled by a volcano during eruption.

lightning A bright flash of light in the sky caused by an electrical discharge from a cloud to Earth or to another cloud.

magma Molten rock that is found deep down beneath the surface of Earth.

mammatus clouds Clouds that look like rounded pouches hanging underneath other clouds, especially cumulonimbus.

mineral A form of chemical found in Earth's crust, often forming crystals.

moment magnitude scale A measure of the energy released by an earthquake, on a scale of 1–10 and abbreviated as "Mw."

Mount Merapi An active, smoking volcano on the island of Java in Indonesia.

mudslide A rapid downhill movement of a large mass of mud formed from loose soil and water.

ocean A large expanse of sea, in particular the Atlantic, Pacific, Indian, Arctic, and Antarctic; or the

entire body of salt water that covers more than 70 percent of Earth's surface.

oil rig A large structure used to house workers and machinery needed to drill wells in the ocean bed and extract oil.

Old Faithful A famous geyser located in Yellowstone National Park in the United States.

pumice A volcanic rock formed when frothy liquid lava is ejected from a volcano and solidifies as it cools.

radar satellite An artificial satellite that monitors weather conditions.

Richter scale A measure of the size of an earthquake – now generally replaced by the moment magnitude scale.

rock A mass of hard consolidated minerals, which forms Earth's crust.

San Andreas Fault A crack in Earth's crust in California, about 800 miles (1,300 km) long, where many earthquakes occur.

sea The masses of salt water that cover more than 70 percent of Earth's surface.

sea level The average height of the sea's surface.

seismic wave Vibrations that travel through the earth as the result of an earthquake or explosion.

seismologist A scientist who studies earthquakes.

seismograph Apparatus for measuring tremors and earthquakes.

soil The surface layers of Earth formed of a mixture of rock particles, minerals, and humus.

SOS message An emergency message sent out by someone needing rescue.

storm A violent disturbance of the atmosphere, often involving strong winds and rain.

supervolcano A volcano capable of producing a massive explosive eruption, which would occur when a huge magma chamber deep under Earth's crust erupted after being under great pressure.

tectonic plates The huge pieces of rock that make up Earth's crust.

tornado A violently destructive windstorm characterized by a funnel-shaped cloud spiraling towards the ground. Also known as a twister.

tsunami A huge destructive wave, caused by a disturbance in the ocean, such as an undersea earthquake or volcanic eruption.

twister see tornado

typhoon The name for a hurricane when it occurs in the northwest Pacific Ocean.

vent An opening in Earth's crust through which magma is expelled during a volcanic eruption.

volcanic ash Bits of powdered rock and glass created by volcanic eruptions.

volcanic bomb A mass of molten rock ejected by a volcano during an eruption which cools into a solid lump before reaching the ground.

volcano A mountain or hill, usually shaped like a cone, that is produced when magma erupts through an opening in the surface of Earth's crust.

weather The condition of rain, sun, and wind at a particular time in a particular place.

weather front The boundary between masses of air of different temperatures.

Yellowstone National Park The first national park in the United States, established in 1872 and located in the states of Wyoming, Montana, and Idaho. The site of one of the world's six known supervolcanoes.

INDEX

PLANET
SOS

PHOTO CREDITS

(t=top, b=bottom, l=left, r=right)

Pg 1 – Bychkov Kirill Alexandrovich / Shutterstock
Pg 2 – Patricia Hofmeester / Shutterstock
Pg 4/5 – Shutterstock
Pg 6 – Jakub Cejpek / Shutterstock
Pg 7 - Juliengrondin/ Shutterstock
Pg 8 – Earthaholic / Shutterstock
Pg 9 – Nathan Chor/ Shutterstock
Pg 10/11 – Dean Cougar / Corbis
Pg 12 – Tom Bean / Corbis
Pg 14 – Reuters / Corbis
Pg 14/15 – Oriontrail / Shutterstock
Pg 16/17 – iBird / Shutterstock
Pg 18 – Shao Quanda/XinHua/Xinhua Press / Corbis
Pg 19 – Christophe Testi / Shutterstock
Pg 20/21 – Mikhail Pogosov / Shutterstock
Pg 20 – Geir Olav Lyngfjell / Shutterstock
Pg 21 - Sascha Corti / Shutterstock
Pg 22 – Celso Diniz / Shutterstock
Pg 23 – (t) atref / Shutterstock, (m) deepspacedave / Shutterstock, (b) Nikolai Tsvetkov / Shutterstock
Pg 24 – Marketa Mark / Shutterstock
Pg 25 – Jack Dagley Photography / Shutterstock
Pg 26 – (t) Graham Taylor / Shutterstock, (b) Joe Gough / Shutterstock
Pg 27 - Eric Gevaert / Shutterstock
Pg 28 – (t) Christopher Waters / Shutterstock, (b) Jeremy Horner / Corbis
Pg 29 – David Hancock / Alamy
Pg 30/31 – 3777190317 / Shutterstock
Pg 32/33 – Tomasz Parys / Shutterstock
Pg 33 – (t) Reuters / Corbis, (b) Kletr / Shutterstock
Pg 34/35 – Kondrachov Vladimir / Shutterstock
Pg 35 - NASA
Pg 36 – (t) Nicholas de Haan / Shutterstock, (b) Kinetic Imagery / Shutterstock
Pg 36/37 – Darko / Shutterstock
Pg 38/39 – Volodymyr / Shutterstock
Pg 40/41 – (t) Reuters / Corbis, (b) 3777190317 / Shutterstock
Pg 41 – Howard Davies / Corbis
Pg 42/43 – Tony Magdaraog / Shutterstock
Pg 43 – (tl) Jagadeesh VN / epa / Corbis, (tr) Suzanne Tucker/ Shutterstock, (b) Creasource / Corbis